**W9-BZR-654**

A DAY IN THE LIFE OF A
Racing Car Mechanic

by Carol Gaskin
Photography by John F. Klein

Troll Associates

Library of Congress Cataloging in Publication Data

Gaskin, Carol.
    A day in the life of a racing car mechanic.

    Summary: Follows a racing car mechanic through his
day as he works on several different projects, including
preparing the car he plans to drive in an upcoming race.
    1. Automobiles, Racing—Maintenance and repair—
Vocational guidance—Juvenile literature. 2. Auto-
mobile mechanics—Juvenile literature. 3. Automobiles,
Racing—Juvenile literature. 4. Dunkel, Brian.
[1. Automobile mechanics. 2. Automobile racing drivers.
3. Occupations. 4. Dunkel, Brian] I. Klein, John F.
(John Frederick), 1950-   , ill. II. Title.
TL236.G37 1985   629.28′78′023   84-2430
ISBN 0-8167-0091-5 (lib. bdg.)
ISBN 0-8167-0092-3 (pbk.)

Copyright © 1985 by Troll Associates, Mahwah, New Jersey.
All rights reserved. No part of this book may be used or
reproduced in any manner whatsoever without written permission
from the publisher.
Printed in the United States of America.

10 9 8 7 6 5 4 3 2 1

The author and publisher wish to thank Brian Dunkel, Frank Resciniti, Louise Richardson, and the rest of the staff at
the Skip Barber Racing School in Canaan, Connecticut.

Brian Dunkel is an auto mechanic at a school for racing car drivers. Besides keeping the school's racing cars in top mechanical condition, Brian sometimes gets to race them. At 8:30 Friday morning, Brian gets his day's assignments from the chief mechanic, Frank.

This morning Brian and Frank will remove a damaged engine from a broken chassis, or car frame. Removing the engine is a job for two people, and it will take at least an hour. Later, Brian may have time to work on the car he will drive in tomorrow's race.

Brian selects the correct tools for the job. He will
need open-end wrenches and socket wrenches. A
mechanic's tools are prized possessions, and it can
take years to build up a complete set. Brian knows
it is important to keep his tools clean and orderly.

Brian and Frank loosen the bolts that hold the engine to the chassis. They have done this many times before, so they know exactly what to do and how to do it. Brian rolls under the car on a mechanic's dolly so he can get at hard-to-reach bolts.

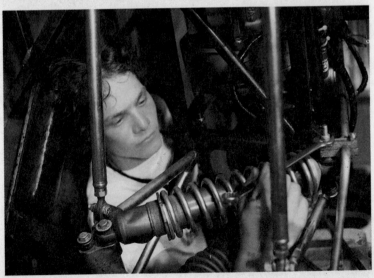

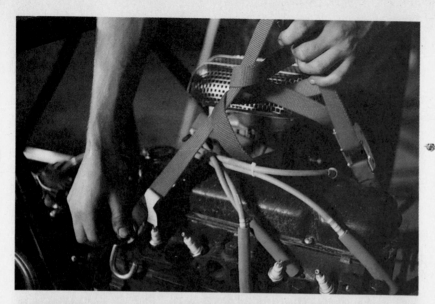

The heavy engine must be lifted on a machine called a hoist. Brian fastens the engine to the hoist with sturdy hooks and a strong belt. Then Frank steadies the engine while Brian pumps a lever, and the engine is hoisted free of the chassis.

The chassis is moved to a welding table. A lower rail has cracked and must be replaced. Frank prepares the new piece as Brian cuts away the broken section and grinds the rough edges smooth. He wears a face shield for protection from flying sparks.

Brian fits the new piece of rail into the gap he has cut, and Frank begins welding it in place. He uses a torch to melt a thin metal rod along the joints where the new and old pieces meet. Dark goggles protect his eyes from the intense light of the torch.

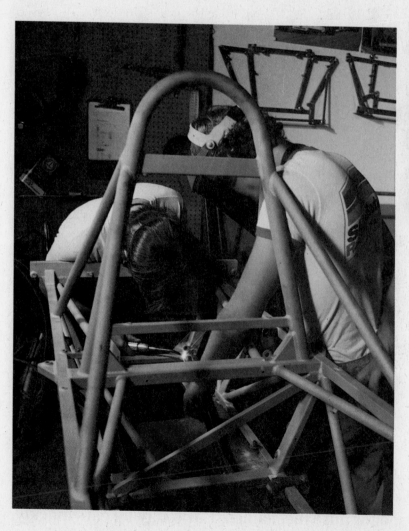

When the job is done, Brian takes time out for lunch. He likes to learn about new developments in his field, so he brings along the latest issue of a magazine for auto mechanics. But today he eats quickly. He is eager to return to his work as he thinks of tomorrow's race.

After lunch, Brian makes his final check on the car he will race tomorrow. He knows that driving skill is important, but the car must also run perfectly. He reaches for his mechanic's checklist. On it are more than twenty steps to be followed in checking the car out.

First Brian tests his engine. He removes the spark plugs and attaches an air hose. He fills the engine with air, then reads a pressure gauge. Brian can diagnose faulty parts—piston rings, intake valves, exhaust valves—if air leaks out where it shouldn't.

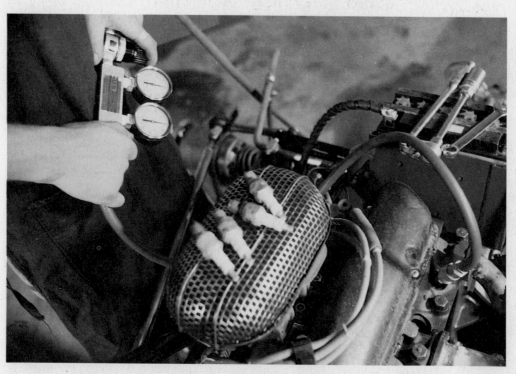

Every test and adjustment a racing car mechanic
makes is designed to help the car go faster. A race
can be won by a fraction of a second, and a single
detail may give a driver the edge he needs to win.
The engine checks out okay.

Brian continues his careful checking. He makes sure each gear engages smoothly before the gearbox is installed, and he checks the springs to make sure they compress at exactly the right rate. He checks the throttle, the brakes, the radiator, the clutch, and every nut and bolt.

When he is satisfied, Brian puts the body on the
car. It comes in two halves, and each half is very
light. Next he bolts on the tires. Racing cars use
special tires with greater traction for high-speed
driving. Brian's car is almost ready.

The last procedure is the alignment. The car must be perfectly balanced. Frank helps Brian set the angles of the wheels, the weight each wheel supports, and the height of the car from the ground. These adjustments are critical for safe driving at high speeds.

After work, Brian walks around the empty race-
track. He looks for landmarks—a sign, a tree
—where he will brake or accelerate in tomorrow's
race. Then he goes home for dinner and a good
night's sleep. He must be rested for the race.

The next morning, the track is still wet from an overnight shower. But it should be dry before the race begins. Brian leaves the "pit lane" to test-drive his car for a few laps. He roars around the track, aware that race officials are timing every lap with a stopwatch.

An official gives Brian a chart with his lap times. Brian has driven well, and he is pleased with his times. But a strange noise he heard during his test drive worries him. There is time to check it out before the race, so he calls his crew together.

When Brian and the crew examine the car, they find a crack in one of the pipes of the exhaust system. The noise of the leaking exhaust told Brian where to look for the problem. The cracked pipe would certainly slow down the car in the race.

Brian's experience as a mechanic has helped him as a driver. No matter how carefully he went over his checklist, he couldn't have found this problem until he drove the car. He knows this repair will help him in today's race.

There is plenty of activity at the track before the race. Crew members drive a fuel truck along the line of cars. Fuel is pumped and tires are changed. Timers ready their charts. Drivers make last-minute checks on their cars or wait their turn on the sidelines.

Brian wears special racing gear—a fireproof suit and gloves, and a helmet with a visor. The driver's seat has been adjusted to give him perfect control of the accelerator, brake, and clutch. Once in the tiny cockpit, Brian practically becomes part of the car.

Brian takes his position on the starting line. He sits quietly and takes a few deep breaths to help him relax. His nervousness disappears as he concentrates on the job ahead of him. The race will last about thirty minutes. Until it is over, Brian's concentration must remain unbroken.

Brian looks up at the judges' stand and listens as the "grid marshal," a track official, announces the start of the race. The drivers are asked to raise their hands to signal that they are ready. One by one, their gloved hands are raised into the air.

A "pace car" leads the drivers once around the track. During this "pace lap," the cars move at a steady speed and maintain their lineup formation. As the pack nears the starting line, the pace car turns off into the pit area. The grid marshal signals the start with a green flag.

The cars take off with a roar. Brian moves up toward the head of the pack. After several laps, he must pass only one more car to take the lead. Ahead of him a yellow flag signals danger, so Brian takes the curve with caution.

Officials at special posts along the track carry walkie-talkies, and they watch for trouble. If a car blows a tire, spins off the track, or spills oil, the nearest official waves a yellow flag. Then those at the other posts do the same. Many accidents are avoided this way.

With just two laps left, Brian sees his chance to pass the leading car on the wide-open part of the track called the "straightaway." In seconds he passes his rival and takes the lead. But there is still one lap to go.

Brian sights each landmark and controls his car through every turn. But as he comes out of the final turn, he knows he could still be overtaken in the last seconds. He quickly accelerates to top speed and roars across the finish line. He wins! He takes the checkered flag!

After the race, Brian is exhilarated—and exhausted. The drivers gather in the pits to trade congratulations and to relive the most exciting moments of the race. For each driver, the time spent behind the wheel has been a unique and valuable learning experience.

Brian realizes that his job provides him with a unique opportunity. First, he gets to use his mechanical skills to repair and maintain the school's fleet of sleek, powerful racing cars. And second, he gets to drive them—and to experience the joy of racing and the thrill of competition!